# FIELD MANUAL
# 100-00

# The Warrior Life:

## What it is and how to live it.

James T. Slattery
Northern Kingdom Publishing
warriorinformation@gmail.com

Based on the Book The Warrior Life

First printed by CreateSpace 10/31/15

ISBN-13:  978-1978222663

ISBN-10:  1978222661

Cover Art:  Crusader Knight's shield.

9th century sword in sheath with a cross-shaped pommel. From the illustrations in the bible of Charles II. Le Chauve (840-887).

Scripture quotations are from the International Standard Version Bible® Copyright © 1996-2010, http://http://isv.org.

Used eSword® Bible Software, Copyright © 2000-2014, for scripture research.  Please support their ministry at http://www.e-sword.net/support.html.

Printed in the United States of America

# Contents

# Introduction

## Exodus 15

[3]The Lord is a warrior;
Yahweh is his name!

It's really very simple – God is a Warrior.

Unfortunately, this Truth is either denied or distorted through the teachings and missions of almost all Christian denominations who have for centuries self-servingly portrayed God as passive, benign, soft, effeminate, maternal, and companion animal friendly who suffers a lot and very deeply with a somewhat manic-depressive personality who endures life with demure passive high-minded acceptance of his woeful Fate.

Where is the One who commanded villages to be wiped-off the face of the earth? Who depopulated entire geographic regions, (including livestock, cats, dogs, and anything else that breathed around them) because they weren't living according to His commandments? Where is the One who threw moneychangers out of the temple overturning their tables and whipping and kicking them to the gutter where they belonged? Where is the One who admonished Mosses by saying, "Why are you crying out to me? Tell the people to get moving". (Exodus 14:15) In other words quit your whining and get it done!

### Hebrews 13

[8]Jesus Christ is the same yesterday and today and forever.

Our Warrior God is the same as He's always been. What has changed is how we perceive Him. Our modern God is less Warrior-like making Him more acceptable to Woman, Children, Sinners, and "Churchmen" who are infinitely more comfortable with a benign feminine socially aware politically correct really-nice God who doesn't hold a grudge and makes you feel better because He's so forgiving of your many foibles. The Truth is God is a Warrior and He's perfect. He's the Alpha and Omega. He's omnipotent and omnipresent and the most powerful being that has ever or will ever exist.

### Revelation 1

[8]I'm the Alpha and the Omega," says the Lord God, "who is, and who was, and who is to come, the Almighty."

God wants you to live the Warrior Life and be fully engaged in the Spiritual Battle between Good and Evil. This requires that you live your life based on scripture while improving yourself intellectually and physically. The scripture based Five Attributes of a Warrior is a structure to organize your Life and direct your intellectual and physical improvement.

**1 Chronicles 12**

[1]The following Men joined Dave at Ziklag while he was hiding from Saul son of Kish. They were among the warriors who fought beside David in Battle. All of them were expert archers, and they could shoot arrows or sling stones with their left hand as well as their right. They were all relatives of Saul from the tribe of Benjamin. Their leader was Ahiezser son of Shemaah from Gibeath; his brother Joash was second-in-command.

…

[8]Some brave and experienced warriors from the tribe of Gad also defected to David while he was at the stronghold in the wilderness. They were experts with both shield and spear, as fierce as lions and as swift as deer on the mountains.

**The Five Attributes of a Warrior:**

1. surrounds himself with Warriors.
2. masters personal protection, weapons, and is physically fit.
3. is mentally tough and perseveres.
4. is wise.
5. serves God above all else.

Before you're promoted to Training Sessions Attendee you should understand a simple concept that has a profound effect on Men causing stress, depression, malaize, etc.

> **Cognitive Dissonance** is the mental stress of discomfort experienced by an individual who holds two or more contrasting beliefs, ideas, or values at the same time, or is confronted by new information that conflicts with existing beliefs, ideas or values.

Cognitive Dissonance occurs when a Man feels compelled to act like a Man but is prevented form doing so by legal, cultural, institutional, and a plethora of other oppositional forces. Not only are Men prevented from acting the way God intended but are forced to act in a way that's counter to their nature. This dissonance is the cause of Men's conscious and unconscious psychological pain.

The Five Attributes of a Warrior will prepare and sustain you in your Spiritual Battle between Good and Evil and either banish or mitigate Cognitive Dissonance.

# Weapons

**Exodus 14:14** "The LORD will fight for you while you keep still."

**Jeremiah 20:11** But the LORD is with me like a fearsome warrior. Therefore, those who pursue me will stumble and won't prevail. They'll be put to great shame, when they don't succeed. Their everlasting disgrace won't be forgotten.

**Deuteronomy 3:18** "Then I commanded you at that time, 'The Lord your God gave you this land as a possession. Those equipped for battle—every Man a warrior—will cross before your fellow Israelis.

**Deuteronomy 10:11** So the LORD told me, 'Get up and proceed to lead the people, so they may enter and take possession of the land that I promised to give their ancestors by an oath.'"

**Judges 5:30** 'They're busy finding and dividing the war booty, aren't they? A girl or two for each valiant warrior, and some dyed materials for Sisera—perhaps dyed, embroidered war booty—or some detailed embroidery for my neck as the booty of war!

**Judges 6:12** The angel of the LORD appeared to him and told him, "The LORD is with you, you valiant warrior!"

**1 Samuel 14:52** There was intense fighting against the Philistines during Saul's entire reign, and whenever Saul discovered a strong or valiant warrior, he would enlist him for service.

**1 Samuel 17:33** Saul told David, "You can't go against this Philistine and fight him. You are only a young Man, but he has been a warrior since his youth."

**2 Samuel 17:8** "You know how strong your father and his Men are. They're as mad as a bear robbed of her cubs! Furthermore, your father is a skilled warrior. He won't stay with his army at night.

**2 Samuel 18:11** Joab asked the Man who was reporting to him, "What! You saw him? Why didn't you kill him right then and there? I would've given you ten pieces of silver and a warrior's sash!"

**Job 16:14** Attack follows attack as he breaks through my defenses! He runs over me like a mighty warrior.

**Psalms 45:3** Strap your sword to your side, mighty warrior, along with your honor and majesty.

**Psalms 76**

⁵Our boldest enemies
    have been plundered.
They lie before us in the
    sleep of death.
    No warrior could left a hand
    against us.
⁶A blast of your
    breath, O God of
    Jacob,
    Their horses and chariots
    lay still.
⁷No wonder you are
    greatly feared.
Who can stand before you
    when your anger explodes?
⁸From heaven you
    sentenced your
    enemies.
the earth tumbled and
    stood silent before
    you.
⁹You stand up to judge
    those who do evil,
    O God,
and to rescue the oppressed from this earth.
¹⁰HuMan defiance only
    enhances your glory,
for you use it as a weapon.

**Psalms 78:65** The LORD awoke as though from sleep, like a mighty warrior stimulated by wine.

**Psalms 89:19** You spoke to your faithful ones through a vision: "I will set a helper over a warrior. I will raise up a chosen one from the people.

**Psalms 120:4** Like a sharp arrow from a warrior, along with fiery coals from juniper trees!

**Psalms 127:4** As arrows in the hand of a warrior, so also are children born during one's youth.

**Proverbs 16:32** Whoever controls his temper is better than a warrior, and anyone who has control of his spirit is better than someone who captures a city.

**Ecclesiastes 3**

¹For everything there is a
                season,
    ³A time to kill and
              a time to heal
  A time to tear down and a
            time to build up

               …

  ⁸A time to love and a time
          to hate.
  A time for war and a time
         for peace.

**Isaiah 3:2** the mighty Man and the warrior, the judge and the prophet, the fortune-teller and the elder,

**Isaiah 42:13** The LORD marches out like a warrior; he stirs up his rage like a Man of war; he makes his anger heard; he shouts aloud; he declares his mastery over his enemies:

**Jerimiah 20:11** But the LORD is with me like a fearsome warrior. Therefore, those who pursue me will stumble and won't prevail. They'll be put to great shame, when they don't succeed. Their everlasting disgrace won't be forgotten.

**Jerimiah 46:12** The nations have heard of your disgrace, and your cry of distress fills the earth. Indeed, one warrior stumbles over another, and both of them fall down together."

**Jerimiah 50:9** Indeed, I'm going to stir up and bring against Babylon a great company of nations from the land of the north. They'll deploy for battle against her, and from there she will be captured. Their arrows will be like a skilled warrior; they won't miss their targets.

**Ezekiel 3:27** "They won't be buried with dead warriors from ancient times, who went straight to Sheol, buried with their war weapons, with their swords placed under their heads and their shields laid on top of their bones, since they spread terror throughout the land of the living.

**Ezekiel 39:20** You'll be fully satiated at my table, dining on horse flesh, horsemen, elite soldiers, and every kind of warrior," declares the Lord GOD.

**Amos 2:14** So the swift runner will not escape, the valiant will not fortify his strength, and the mighty warrior will not save his life.

**Zechariah 9:13** For I have bent Judah as if it were my bow, loading it with Ephraim. I raised up your sons, Zion, against your sons, Greece, wielding you like a mighty warrior's sword.

**Matthew 10:34** "Do not think that I came to bring peace on earth. I did not come to bring peace but a sword!

# Training Session 1: A Warrior Surrounds Himself with Warriors

## Jeremiah 20

[11]But the Lord stands beside me like a great warrior.

**Focus of Training:**

1. Why should a Warrior surround himself with Warriors?

2. How do other Warriors support and strengthen us?

3. How do others weaken us?

4. Since God is a Warrior how does he support and strengthen us?

5. How do you identify and find other Warriors?

# Weapons

**Leviticus 25:35** If your relative becomes poor so that he is indebted to you, then you are to support him. You are to let him live with you just like the resident alien and the traveler.

**2 Samuel 10:11** He said, "If the Arameans prove too strong for me, then you are to help me. If the Ammonites prove too strong for you, then I will come help you.

**2 Samuel 19:14** By doing things like this, he persuaded all the Men of Judah to unite in support of him. They sent the king this message: "Come on back, you and all of your army!"

**2 Samuel 22:3** He is my God, my strong stone—in him I will find my refuge—my shield, the strength of my salvation, my high tower, my way of escape, and the one who is saving me. You will save me from violence.

**2 Samuel 22:19** They confronted me when I was in trouble, but the LORD remained my support!

**1 Kings 1:7** He had the support of Zeruiah's son Joab and of Abiathar the priest, who followed Adonijah and assisted him,

**2 Chronicles 13:7** Useless troublemakers soon gathered around him, who turned out to be too strong for Rehoboam, because he was young, timid, and unable to withstand them.

**2 Chronicles 16:9** The LORD's eyes keep on roaming throughout the earth, looking for those whose hearts completely belong to him, so that he may strongly support them.

**Psalms 16:5** The LORD is my inheritance and my cup; you support my lot.

**Psalms 18:18** They confronted me in the day of my calamity, but the LORD was my support.

**Psalms 80:17** May you support the Man at your right hand; the son of Man whom you have raised for yourself.

**Proverbs 27:17** Iron sharpens iron; so a Man sharpens a friend's character.

**Ecclesiastes 4:12** If someone attacks one of them, the two of them together will resist. Furthermore, the tri-braided cord is not soon broken.

**Isaiah 42:1** "Here is my servant, whom I support, my chosen one, in whom I delight. I've placed my Spirit upon him; and he'll deliver his justice throughout the world.

**Isaiah 63:5** I looked, but there was no helper, I was appalled that there was no one to give support; so my own arm brought me victory, and as for my wrath, it supported me.

**Acts 20:34** You yourselves know that I worked with my own hands to support myself and those who were with me.

**1 Peter 5:9** Resist him and be firm in the faith, because you know that your brothers throughout the world are undergoing the same kinds of suffering.

**1 Peter 5:10** After you have suffered for a little while, the God of all grace, who called you by the Messiah Jesus to his eternal glory, will restore you, establish you, strengthen you, and support you.

**3 John 1:8** Therefore, we ought to support such people so that we can become genuine helpers with them.

**Matthew 14:30** But when he noticed the strong wind, he was frightened. As he began to sink, he shouted, "Lord, save me!"

# Training Session 2:  A Warrior Masters Personal Protection, Weapons, and is Physically Fit

## Matthew 10

[16]You see, I am sending you out like sheep among wolves.
So be as cunning as serpents and as innocent as doves.

**Focus of Training:**

1. Why are mastering Personal Protection, Weapons, and being Physically Fit Warrior attributes?

2. Why are they important?

3. How will they contribute to the Spiritual Battle between Good and Evil?

4. What does it mean to "Work to Your Limitations"?

5. What are your Warrior skills and abilities?

# Weapons

**Numbers 1:2** "Take a census of the entire Israeli community, numbering them by their tribes and by ancestral houses. List the names of every male one-by-one, 3  from 20 years and upward. You and Aaron are to register everyone in Israel who is able to go to war, company by company.

**2 Samuel 22:31** This God! His way is perfect! What the LORD declares proves true. He shields everyone who flees for protection to him!

**Psalms 141:8** Nevertheless, my eyes are on you, Lord GOD, as I seek protection in you. Don't leave me defenseless!

**Ecclesiastes 7:12** Indeed, wisdom gives protection, just like money does, but it's better to know that wisdom gives life, to those who have mastered it.

**Genesis 27:3** so go find your weapons, take your bow and arrows, go outside, and hunt some game for me.

**Judges 18:11** So 600 descendants of Dan from Zorah and Eshtaol set out for battle, armed with military weapons.

**Judges 18:16** While the 600 Danite soldiers, armed with military weapons, stood guard at the entrance to the gate,

**Judges 18:17** the five Men who had gone to scout out the land arrived, entered Micah's home and took possession of the carved image, the ephod, the household idols, and the cast image. Meanwhile, the priest stood outside by the entrance to the gate with the 600 Men armed with military weapons.

**1 Samuel 17:54** David took the Philistine's head and brought it to Jerusalem, but he put Goliath's weapons in his tent.

**1 Samuel 21:8** David told Ahimelech, "Is there no spear or sword available here? I took neither my sword nor my weapons with me, because the king's mission is urgent."

**1 Samuel 31:9** They cut off his head and stripped him of his weapons. They sent people throughout the territory of the Philistines to report the good news in the temples of their idols and to the people.

**1 Samuel 31:10** They put Saul's weapons in the temple of Asherah and fastened his corpse to the wall of Beth-shan.

**2 Samuel 1:27** How the valiant have fallen! How the weapons of war are destroyed!"

**2 Samuel 22:18** He rescued me from my strong enemy—from those who continually hate me, since they were stronger than I.

**2 Samuel 23:10** but Eleazar remained standing right where he was and fought so hard against the Philistines that he became exhausted—he couldn't even let go of his sword! The LORD magnificently delivered them that day. After Eleazar had won the battle, the other soldiers returned, but only to strip the weapons and armor from the dead.

**2 Kings 11:8** guarding the king and surrounding him with weapons in hand. Whoever comes within range is to be killed. Stay with the king wherever he goes, coming or going."

**2 Kings 11:11** So the guards stood assembled, every soldier with weapons in hand, surrounding the king from the right side corner of the Temple to the left side corner, including around the altar and the Temple.

**1 Chronicles 19:12** He told Abishai, "If the Arameans prove too strong for me, then you are to help me. If the Ammonites prove too strong for you, then I will help you.

**2 Chronicles 23:7** The descendants of Levi will surround the king, brandishing weapons in their hands, and anybody who enters the Temple will be killed. Stay near the king wherever he enters and leaves."

**2 Chronicles 23:10** He set the rest of the people to serve as guards for the king, and each one brandished weapons in his hand, from the south side of the Temple to the north side of the Temple, around the altar, and surrounding the palace.

**2 Chronicles 32:5** Hezekiah took courage and rebuilt all of the walls that had been broken down. Then he erected watch towers on them, and added another external wall. He fortified the terrace ramparts in the city of David and prepared a large number of weapons and shields.

**Job 39:21** He paws the ground in the valley and rejoices in his strength; he goes out to face weapons.

**Psalms 7:13** He prepares weapons of death for himself, he makes his arrows into fiery shafts.

**Psalms 76:3** There he shattered sharp arrows, shields, swords, and weapons of war.

**Song of Solomon 4:4** Your neck is like the tower of David, built with rows of stones. A thousand shields are hung upon it, all the weapons of the warriors.

**Isaiah 13:5** They're coming from a faraway land, from the distant horizon—the LORD and the weapons of his anger—to destroy the entire land."

**Jerimiah 21:4** 'This is what the LORD God of Israel says: "I'm about to turn against you the weapons of war that are in your hands and with which you are fighting the king of Babylon and the Chaldeans who are besieging you outside the walls. I'll gather them into the center of this city.

**Jerimiah 22:7** I'll appoint people to destroy you, Men with their weapons. They'll cut down some of your choice cedars and throw them into the fire.

**Jerimiah 50:25** The LORD will open his armory, and bring out the weapons of his anger. Indeed, a work of the Lord GOD of the Heavenly Armies will be in the land of the Chaldeans.

**Jerimiah 51:20** "You are my war-club and weapons of war. I'll smash nations with you and destroy kingdoms with you.

**Ezekiel 23:24** "'They'll invade you with weapons, chariots, wagons, and a vast army. They'll set themselves in place to attack you from every direction with large shields, small shields, and helmet. I'll turn over judgment to them, and they'll punish you according to their own standards.

**Ezekiel 32:12** I'm going to make your gangs die using the weapons of valiant warriors, all of whom are ruthless people. They will devastate the majesty of Egypt, destroying all of its hordes.

**Ezekiel 32:27** "They won't be buried with dead warriors from ancient times, who went straight to Sheol, buried with their war weapons, with their swords placed under their heads and their shields laid on top of their bones, since they spread terror throughout the land of the living.

**Ezekiel 33:26** You keep trusting in your weapons, you continue to commit loathsome deeds, Men keep defiling their neighbors' wives, and you're going to take possession of the land?

**Ezekiel 39:9** "After all this happens, the people who live in the cities of Israel will be kindling fires for seven years, using small shields, large shields, bows, arrows, clubs, personal weapons, and spears to do so.

**Ezekiel 39:10** They won't need to cut down trees from the fields nor gather firewood from the forests, because they will light fires with the weapons as they plunder the plunderers and loot the looters!" declares the Lord GOD.

**Zechariah 9:10** I will banish chariots from Ephraim and horses from Jerusalem. War weapons will be banished, and your king will speak peace to the nations. His dominion will extend from sea to sea, and from the River to the farthest portion of the earth.

**John 18:3** So Judas took a detachment of soldiers and some officers from the high priests and the Pharisees and went there with lanterns, torches, and weapons.

**2 Corinthians 10:4** For the weapons of our warfare are not those of the world. Instead, they have the power of God to demolish fortresses. We tear down arguments.

**Luke 12:40** So be ready, because the Son of Man is coming at a time when you don't expect him."

**Luke 19:43** because the days will come when your enemies will build walls around you, surround you, and close you in on every side.

# Training Session 3:  A Warrior Is Mentally Tough and Perseveres

## Joseph 1

[9]"I've commanded you, haven't I?  Be strong and courageous.  Don't be fearful or discouraged, because the Lord your God is with you wherever you go." beside me like a great warrior

**Focus of Training:**

1.   What does it mean to be Mentally Tough?

2.   What is Perseverance?

3.   How is our Mental Toughness and Perseverance compromised?

4.   Why is it important for a Warrior to be Mentally Tough and to Persevere?

5.   What are ways to develop Mental Toughness and Perseverance?

# Weapons

**Genesis 19:13** because we're going to destroy it. The LORD knows how their behavior stinks, so he sent us here to destroy it!

**Deuteronomy 31:29** because I know that after my death, you'll surely act wickedly and turn from the road that I've instructed you. As a result, evil will fall on you in days to come, because you'll act wickedly in the sight of the LORD, causing him to become angry due to your behavior."

**1 Chronicles 21:7** God considered this behavior to be evil, so he attacked Israel.

**Ezra 9:13** "After all that has happened to us because of our evil behavior, and because of our great sin—considering that you our God have punished us less than our iniquities deserve and have given us this deliverance—

**Job 23:10** Because he knows the road on which I travel, when he had tested me, I'll come out like gold.

**Job 34:11** because he repays a person for his behavior; and according to a person's conduct, he lets it happen to him.

**Job 34:21** Yes, Job, his eyes constantly watch the behavior of human beings; he carefully observes their every step.

**Job 34:25** Thus he acknowledges their behavior, and overcomes them; when night time comes, they are crushed.

**Psalms 119:9** Bet. How can a young Man keep his behavior pure? By guarding it in accordance with your word.

**Proverbs 1:3** for acquiring the discipline that produces wise behavior, righteousness, justice, and upright living;

**Proverbs 7:25** Don't be led astray by her lifestyle, and don't imitate her behavior.

**Proverbs 14:14** The faithless one will pay for his behavior, but a good Man will be rewarded for his.

**Proverbs 21:8** The conduct of a guilty Man is perverse, but the behavior of the pure is upright.

**Isaiah 1:16** "Wash yourselves, and make yourselves clean; remove your evil behavior from my presence; stop practicing what is evil.

**Isaiah 48:10** Look, I have refined you, but not like silver; I have purified you in the furnace of affliction.

**Jeremiah 13:27** I've seen your detestable behavior: your adulteries, your passionate neighing, your lewd immorality on the hills in the field. How terrible it will be for you, Jerusalem! You are unclean. How much longer will this go on?"

**Jeremiah 35:15** I've sent you all my servants, the prophets, sending them again and again. I've said, 'Each of you turn from his evil behavior and make your deeds right. Don't follow other gods to serve them. Then you will remain in the land that I gave to you and to your ancestors. But you haven't paid attention and you haven't obeyed me.

**Ezekiel 3:18** "So when I say to a wicked person, 'You're about to die,' if you don't warn or instruct that wicked person that his behavior is wicked so he can live, that wicked person will die in his sin, but I'll hold you responsible for his death.

**Ezekiel 3:19** If you warn the wicked person, and he doesn't repent of his wickedness or of his wicked behavior, he'll die in his sin, but you will have saved your own life."

**Ezekiel 5:9** In fact, I'm going to do what I've never done before and what I'll never again do, because of all of your loathsome behavior:

**Ezekiel 7:8** "Very soon now, I'll pour out my burning anger on you. I'll complete expressing my anger at you, judge you according to your behavior, and repay you for all your detestable practices.

**Ezekiel 7:9** I won't be showing pity or compassion. I'll repay you according to your behavior while your detestable practices remain among you. And you'll know that I, the LORD, have been attacking you.

**Ezekiel 7:27** "The king will mourn, the prince will be clothed with desolation, and the hands of the people of the land will tremble. I'll deal with them according to their behavior and I will judge them by how they've judged. Then they'll learn that I am the LORD."

**Ezekiel 11:21** But to those whose hearts delight in loathsome things and detestable practices, I'll bring the consequences of their behavior crashing down on their own heads," declares the Lord GOD.'"

**Ezekiel 13:22** "Because you've dismayed the heart of the righteous—whom I never intended to dismay—with lies, and because you've encouraged the wicked so that he wouldn't abandon his evil behavior and by doing so live,

**Ezekiel 16:43** Because you didn't remember the time when you were young, but instead you provoked me to anger because of all these things, watch out! I'm going to bring your behavior back to haunt you!" declares the Lord GOD. "Didn't you do this wicked thing, in addition to all your other detestable practices?"

**Ezekiel 16:47** It wasn't just that you lived like they did and committed their detestable practices, but in just a little while your behavior led you to become more corrupt than they were!"

**Ezekiel 16:61** Then you'll remember your behavior and be ashamed when you greet your sisters— your elder sister and your younger sister. I'll give them to you as daughters, but not on account of my covenant with you.

**Ezekiel 18:25** "Yet you keep saying, 'The LORD isn't being consistent with his standards.' Pay attention, you house of Israel: Is my behavior really inconsistent with my standards? Isn't it your behavior that isn't just?

**Ezekiel 18:27** When a wicked person quits his wicked behavior and does what's just and right, he'll be enabled to live.

**Ezekiel 18:30** "Therefore, Israel, I'm going to judge you according to the behavior of each and every one of you," declares the Lord GOD. "So repent and turn from all your sins so that sin won't keep on being a stumbling block for you.

**Ezekiel 22:31** so I poured my indignation over them. With my fierce anger, I've consumed them. I brought the consequences of their behavior upon them,' declares the Lord GOD."

**Ezekiel 28:15** You were blameless in your behavior from the day you were created until wickedness was discovered in you.

**Ezekiel 33:8** If I should say to a certain wicked person, "You wicked Man, you're certainly about to die," but you don't warn him to turn from his wicked behavior, he'll die in his guilt, but I'll seek retribution for his bloodshed from you.

**Ezekiel 33:9** However, if you warn the wicked to turn from his behavior and he does not do so, he will die in his guilt, and you will have saved yourself.'"

**Hosea 4:9** So it will be: like people, like priest. I will punish them for their lifestyles, rewarding them according to their behavior.

**Micah 7:13** The land will become desolate because of its inhabitants, and as a result of their behavior.

**Galatians 2:13** The other Jews also joined him in this hypocritical behavior, to the extent that even Barnabas was caught up in their hypocrisy.

**1 Timothy 4:12** Do not let anyone look down on you because you are young, but be an example for other believers in your speech, behavior, love, faithfulness, and purity.

**Malachi 3:3** He will sit refining and purifying silver, purifying the descendants of Levi, refining them like gold and silver. Then they'll bring a righteous offering to the LORD.

**1 Peter 1:6** You greatly rejoice in this, even though you have to suffer various kinds of trial for a little while, [7]so that your genuine faith, which is more valuable than gold that perishes when tested by fire, may result in praise, glory, and honor when Jesus, the Messiah, is revealed.

**Exodus 1:7** But the Israelis were fruitful and increased abundantly. They multiplied in numbers and became very, very strong. As a result, the land was filled with them.

**Numbers 13:18** See what the land is like. Observe whether the people who live there are strong or weak, or whether they're few or numerous.

**Numbers 13:28** except that the people who have settled in the land are strong, and their cities are greatly fortified. We also saw the descendants of Anak.

**Numbers 13:31** "We can't attack those people," the Men who were with him said, "because they're too strong compared to us."

**Numbers 21:24** But Israel defeated him in battle and took possession of all his lands from Arnon to Jabbok, including the Ammonites, even though the border of the Ammonites was strong.

**Deuteronomy 2:36** From Aroer on the edge of Arnon Valley and from the town all the way to Gilead, there was no city that was too strong for us—the LORD our God delivered them all to us.

**Deuteronomy 3:28** Therefore charge Joshua to be doubly strong, for he will lead this people and cause them to inherit the land that you'll see.'

**Deuteronomy 9:2** The Anakim are strong and tall, and you know them. You've heard it said, 'Who can stand up against the Anakim?'

**Deuteronomy 11:8** "Keep all the commands that I'm giving you today, so you can be strong enough to enter and possess the land that you are crossing over to inherit

**Deuteronomy 14:26** You may spend the money to your heart's content to buy livestock, flocks, wine, strong drink, and whatever you desire. You and your household may eat there and rejoice in the presence of the LORD your God."

**Deuteronomy 31:6** Be strong and courageous. Don't fear or tremble before them, because the LORD your God will be the One who keeps on walking with you—he won't leave you or abandon you."

**Deuteronomy 31:7** Then Moses called on Joshua and told him in the presence of everyone in Israel, "Be strong and courageous, because you'll bring this people to the land that the LORD your God had promised to give your ancestors. You will be the one who causes them to possess it.

**Deuteronomy 31:23** Then the LORD charged Nun's son Joshua, "Be strong and courageous, because you'll bring the Israelis to the land that I promised to them by an oath. I'll be with you."

**Deuteronomy 34:7** Moses was 120 years old when he died. His eyesight wasn't impaired and he was still vigorous and strong.

**Joshua 1:6** "Be strong and courageous, because you'll be leading this people to inherit the land that I promised to give their ancestors.

**Joshua 1:7** Only be strong and very courageous to ensure that you obey all the instructions that my servant Moses gave you—turn neither to the right nor to the left from it—so that you may succeed wherever you go.

**Joshua 1:9** "I've commanded you, haven't I? Be strong and courageous. Don't be fearful or discouraged, because the LORD your God is with you wherever you go."

**Joshua 1:18** Anyone who rebels against what you say and doesn't listen to your words regarding everything that you command will be executed. Only be strong and courageous."

**Joshua 4:24** Do this so that all of the people of the earth may know how strong the power of the LORD is, and so that you may fear the LORD your God every day."

**Joshua 10:25** Joshua told the army, "Don't fear or be dismayed! Be strong and courageous, because this is how the LORD will treat all of your enemies whom you fight."

**Joshua 14:11** I'm still as strong today as I was the day Moses commissioned me. I'm as strong today as I was then, and I can go out to battle and come back successful.

**Joshua 17:13** Later on, when the Israelis had become strong, they forced the Canaanites to work for them, but they never did expel them completely.

**Joshua 17:18** but the hill country will also belong to you. Even though it's a forest, you will clear it and possess it to its farthest borders. You'll drive out the Canaanites, even though they have iron chariots and even though they're strong."

**Joshua 23:6** "Stand very strong, then, so you can obey and carry out everything written in the Book of the Law of Moses, turning neither to the right nor to the left of it.

**Joshua 23:9** because the LORD has expelled great and strong nations ahead of you. Now as for you, not a single Man has been able to oppose you right to this day.

**Judges 1:28** When Israel had grown strong, they subjected the Canaanites to conscripted labor and never did expel them completely.

**Judges 1:35** Furthermore, the Amorites continued to inhabit Mount Heres in Aijalon and Shaalbim. Eventually, however, after the tribe of Joseph had become strong, the Amorites were subjected to conscripted labor.

**Judges 3:10** The Spirit of the LORD was on him, and he governed Israel. When Othniel went out to battle, the LORD handed king Cushan-rishathaim of Aram-naharaim into his control, and Othniel's domination of Cushan-rishathaim was strong.

**Judges 3:29** At that time they attacked about 10,000 Moabites, all of whom were strong and valiant Men. Not one Man escaped.

**Judges 13:24** Later on, the Woman gave birth to a son and named him Samson. The child grew strong and the LORD blessed him.

**Judges 18:26** Then the descendants of Dan went on their way. Because Micah saw that they were too strong for him, he turned and went back home.

**1 Samuel 4:9** Philistines, be strong and be Men, or you will become slaves to the Hebrews just as they have been slaves to you! Be Men and fight!"

**1 Samuel 14:52** There was intense fighting against the Philistines during Saul's entire reign, and whenever Saul discovered a strong or valiant warrior, he would enlist him for service.

**1 Samuel 23:13** David and his Men, about 600 strong, got up and left Keilah. They moved around wherever they could go. Saul was advised that David had escaped from Keilah, so he stopped the campaign.

**2 Samuel 3:1** After this, a state of protracted war existed between Saul's dynasty and David's dynasty, and the dynasty of David continued to grow and become strong while the dynasty of Saul continued to grow weaker.

**2 Samuel 10:12** Be strong, be courageous on behalf of our people and for the cities of our God, and may the LORD do what he thinks is best."

**2 Samuel 17:8** "You know how strong your father and his Men are. They're as mad as a bear robbed of her cubs! Furthermore, your father is a skilled warrior. He won't stay with his army at night.

**1 Kings 2:2** "I'm headed down the road that everyone who lives on earth travels, so be strong and demonstrate that you're a grown Man

**1 Chronicles 11:10** These are the leaders of the elite warriors who were strong supporters of David in his kingdom, along with all of Israel, in keeping with the message from the LORD concerning Israel.

**1 Corinthians 19:13** Be strong, be courageous on behalf of our people and for the cities of our God, and may the LORD do what he thinks is best."

**1 Corinthians 22:13** Then you will be successful, if you keep on observing the statutes and ordinances that the LORD commanded Moses concerning Israel. Be strong, be courageous, and never give in to fear or dismay.

**1 Corinthians 28:10** So keep watching, because the LORD has chosen you to build the Temple of his sanctuary. So be strong, and get to work!"

**1 Corinthians 28:20** David continued with these words for his son Solomon: "Be strong and courageous, and get to work. Never be afraid or discouraged, for the LORD God, my God, is with you. He will not fail you nor will he abandon you right up to your completion of the work for the service of the Temple of the LORD.

**1 Corinthians 29:12** Both wealth and honor proceed from you, and you are ruling over them all. You control power—you control who is made great, and how everyone becomes strong.

**2 Chronicles 15:7** Now as for you, be strong and never be discouraged, because there will be reward for your work."

**2 Chronicles 22:9** Jehu also searched for Ahaziah, had him apprehended while Ahaziah was hiding out in Samaria, and had Ahaziah brought to him. Jehu had Ahaziah executed and buried. It was said of Jehu, "He is the son of Jehoshaphat, who sought the LORD with all of his heart." As a result, there was no one left in the household of Ahaziah strong enough to reign in the kingdom.

**2 Chronicles 26:15** He also had various siege engines built by skilled designers and placed them on the towers and on the corner ramparts that could fire arrows and very large stones. His reputation spread far and wide, and he was marvelously assisted until he grew very strong.

**2 Chronicles 26:16** But after he had become strong, in his arrogance he acted corruptly and became unfaithful to the LORD his God, and he dared to enter the LORD's Temple to burn incense on the incense altar.

**2 Chronicles 32:7** "Be strong and courageous. Don't be afraid or disheartened because of the king of Assyria or because of the army that accompanies him, because the one who is with us is greater than the one with him.

**Ezra 9:12** So, therefore, do not give your daughters in marriage to their sons, nor marry their daughters to your sons, and under no circumstances are you to seek their well-being or their wealth, so that you may remain strong, enjoying the best things the land has to give, and so that you may establish an inheritance for your children forever.'

**Ezra 10:4** So get up—it's your responsibility! We're with you. Be strong, and get to work."

**Nehemiah 1:10** These are your servants as well as your people, whom you have redeemed by your great power and by your strong hand.

**Job 6:12** Am I as strong as a rock? Am I some kind of iron Man?

**Job 9:4** He is wise in heart and strong in will—who can be stubborn against him and succeed?

**Job 18:7** His strong steps are restricted, and his own advice trips him up.

**Job 24:22** God prolongs the life of the strong by his power, but they get up in the morning without purpose in life.

**Job 36:5** "Indeed God is mighty and he doesn't show disrespect; he is mighty and strong of heart.

**Job 39:4** Their young are strong; they grow up in the open field; then they go off and don't return to them."

**Job 40:18** His bones are conduits of bronze; his strong bones are like bars of iron.

**Job 41:24** His heart is as strong as stone, it is as hard as a lower millstone.

**Psalms 18:17** He delivered me from my strong enemies, from those who hated me because they were stronger than I.

**Psalms 21:13** Rise up, LORD, because you are strong; we will sing and praise your power.

**Psalms 24:8** Who is the King of Glory? The LORD strong and mighty, the LORD, mighty in battle.

**Psalms 30:7** By your favor, LORD, you established me as a strong mountain; Then you hid your face, and I was dismayed.

**Psalms 31:24** Be strong, and let your heart be courageous, all you who put your hope in the LORD.

**Psalms 40:4** How blessed is that strong person who places his trust in the LORD, and who has not acknowledged the proud nor resorted to lies.

**Psalms 45:4** In your majesty ride forth for the cause of truth, humility, and righteousness; and your strong right hand will teach you awesome things.

**Psalms 62:7** I rely on God who is my deliverance and my glory; he is my strong rock, and my refuge is in God.

**Psalms 71:7** I have become an example to many that you are my strong refuge.

**Psalms 89:13** Your arm is strong; your hand is mighty; indeed, your right hand is victorious.

**Psalms 136:12** with a strong hand and an active arm, for his gracious love is everlasting.

**Psalms 140:7** LORD, my Lord, my strong deliverer, you have protected my head in the time of battle.

**Psalms 142:6** Pay attention to my cry, for I have been brought very low. Deliver me from my tormentors, for they are far too strong for me.

**Psalms 144:2** he is my gracious love and my fortress, my strong tower and my deliverer, my shield and the one in whom I find refuge, who subdues peoples under me.

**Proverbs 4:3** When I was a son to my father, not yet strong and an only son to my mother,

**Proverbs 6:34** because jealousy incites a strong Man's rage, and he will show no mercy when it's time for revenge.

**Proverbs 18:10** The name of the LORD is a strong tower; a righteous person rushes to it and is lifted up above the danger.

**Proverbs 18:18** Casting dice settles a dispute, deciding between strong contenders.

**Proverbs 23:11** for strong is their Redeemer who will take up their case against you.

**Proverbs 24:5** A wise Man is strong, and a knowledgeable Man grows in strength.

**Ecclesiastes 9:11** I considered and observed on earth the following: The race doesn't go to the swift, nor the battle to the strong, nor food to the wise, nor wealth to the smart, nor recognition to the skilled. Instead, timing and circumstances meet them all.

**Ecclesiastes 12:3** when that day comes, the palace guards will tremble, strong Men will stoop down, Women grinders will cease because they are few, and the sight of those who peer through the lattice will grow dim.

**Song of Solomon 8:6** Set me like a seal over your heart, like a seal on your arm. For love is as strong as death, passion as intense as Sheol. The flames of love are flames of fire, a blaze that comes from the LORD.

**Isaiah 5:22** "How terrible it will be for those who are heroes at drinking wine, and champions in mixing strong drink,

**Isaiah 17:4** "At that time, Jacob's glory will have become weakened, and his strong flesh will turn gaunt;

**Isaiah 25:3** Therefore strong peoples will glorify you; cities of ruthless nations will revere you.

**Isaiah 26:1** At that time, people will sing this song in the land of Judah: "We have a strong city; God crafts victory, its walls and ramparts.

**Isaiah 28:2** Look! The LORD has one who is mighty and strong, like a hailstorm and destructive tempest, like a storm of mighty, overflowing water—and he will give rest to the land.

**Isaiah 28:7** These people also stagger from wine and reel from strong drink. Priests and prophets stagger from strong drink; they're drunk from wine; they reel from strong drink, waver when seeing visions, and stumble when rendering decisions.

**Isaiah 29:9** "Act stupid! Be astonished! Act blind, and be blind! Be drunk, but not from wine; stagger around, but not from strong drink.

**Isaiah 31:1** "How terrible it will be for those who go down to Egypt for help, who rely on horses, who trust in the chariot, because there are so many, and in charioteers, because they are so strong— but do not look to the Holy One of Israel or seek the LORD!

**Isaiah 35:4** Say to those with anxious hearts, 'Be strong, do not be afraid! Here is your God—he will bring vengeance, he will bring divine retribution, and he will save you.'

**Isaiah 41:6** Each helps his neighbor, saying to each other, 'Be strong!'

**Isaiah 53:12** Therefore I will allot him a portion with the great, and he will divide the spoils with the strong; because he poured out his life to death, and was numbered with the transgressors; yet he carried the sins of many, and made intercession for their transgressions."

**Jeremiah 9:23** This is what the LORD says: "The wise Man is not to boast in his wisdom; the strong Man is not to boast in his strength; and the rich Man is not to boast in his riches.

**Jeremiah 14:9** Why are you like a Man taken by surprise, like a strong Man who can't deliver? You are among us, LORD, and your name is the one by which we're called. Don't abandon us!

**Jeremiah 21:5** Because of my anger, wrath, and great fury, I'll fight against you myself with an outstretched hand and a strong arm.

**Jeremiah 32:21** By your strong hand and outstretched arm, and with great terror, you brought your people Israel out of the land of Egypt with signs and wonders.

**Jeremiah 48:14** "How can you say, 'We're strong warriors, and soldiers ready for battle'?

**Ezekiel 2:4** They're stubborn and strong willed. I'm sending you to them to tell them what the LORD says.

**Ezekiel 22:14** Can your heart stand up to this? Can your hands remain strong when I deal with you? I, the LORD, have spoken and will fulfill this.

**Daniel 2:42** Just as their toes and feet are part iron and part clay, so will the kingdom be both strong and brittle.

**Daniel 4:22** it's you, your majesty! You've become great and strong, your greatness has grown to the heavens, and your dominion reaches to the distant parts of the earth.

**Daniel 10:19** and said, 'Don't be afraid, Man highly regarded. Be at peace, and be strong.' "As soon as he spoke to me, I gained strength and replied, 'Sir, please speak, now that you've strengthened me.'

**Daniel 11:5** "'The southern king will become strong, along with one of his officials, who will become stronger than he and rule over his own realm with great power.

**Daniel 11:32** Through flattery he'll corrupt those who act wickedly toward the covenant, but people who know their God will be strong and take action.

**Joel 1:6** Indeed, a nation has invaded my land—it is strong and its population is too large to count—with teeth like a lion and fangs like a lioness.

**Joel 2:2** A day of doom and gloom, a day of clouds and shadows like the dawn spreads out to cover the mountains—a people strong and robust. Never has there been anything like it, neither will anything follow to compare with it, even through the lifetime of generation upon generation."

**Nahum 3:14** Draw water, because a siege is coming! Strengthen your fortresses! Make the clay good and strong! Mix the mortar! Go get your brick molds!

**Haggai 2:4** Now be strong, Zerubbabel,' declares the LORD, 'and be strong, Joshua son of Jehozadak, the high priest, and be strong, all you people of the land,' declares the LORD. 'Go to work, because I am with you,' declares the LORD of the Heavenly Armies.

**Zechariah 8:9** "This is what the LORD of the Heavenly Armies says: 'Be strong so the Temple can be built, you who are now listening to this message spoken by the prophets when the foundation was laid to the Temple of the LORD of the Heavenly Armies.

**Matthew 12:29** How can someone go into a strong Man's house and carry off his possessions without first tying up the strong Man? Then he can ransack his house.

**Luke 1:15** because he will be great in the Lord's presence. He will never drink wine or any strong drink, and he will be filled with the Holy Spirit even before he is born.

**Luke 1:80** Now the child continued to grow and to become spiritually strong. He lived in the wilderness until the day he appeared in Israel.

**Luke 11:21** "When a strong Man, fully armed, guards his own Mansion, his property is safe.

**Romans 1:11** For I am longing to see you so that I may impart to you some spiritual gift to make you strong,

**Romans 15:1** Now we who are strong ought to be patient with the weaknesses of those who are not strong and must stop pleasing ourselves.

**1 Corinthians 1:8** He will keep you strong until the end, so that you will be blameless on the Day of our Lord Jesus the Messiah.

**1 Corinthians 4:10** We are fools for the Messiah's sake, but you are wise in the Messiah. We are weak, but you are strong. You are honored, but we are dishonored.

**1 Corinthians 16:13** Remain alert. Keep standing firm in your faith. Keep on being courageous and strong.

**2 Corinthians 12:10** That is why I take such pleasure in weaknesses, insults, hardships, persecutions, and difficulties for the Messiah's sake, for when I am weak, then I am strong.

**2 Corinthians 13:9** We are glad when we are weak and you are strong. That is what we are praying for—your maturity.

**Ephesians 6:10** Finally, be strong in the Lord, relying on his mighty strength.

**1 Thessalonians 2:2** As you know, we suffered persecution and were mistreated in Philippi. Yet we were encouraged by our God to tell you his gospel in spite of strong opposition.

**1 Thessalonians 3:13** Then your hearts will be strong, blameless, and holy in the presence of God, who is our Father, when our Lord Jesus appears with all his saints.

**1 Timothy 4:16** Pay close attention to your life and your teaching. Persevere in these things, because if you do so, you will save both yourself and those who listen to you.

**2 Timothy 2:1** As for you, my child, be strong by the grace that is in the Messiah Jesus.

**James 3:4** And look at ships! They are so big that it takes strong winds to drive them, yet they are steered by a tiny rudder wherever the helmsman directs.

**1 John 2:14** I have written to you, little children, because you have known the Father. I have written to you, fathers, because you have known the one who has existed from the beginning. I have written to you, young people, because you are strong and because God's word remains in you and you have overcome the evil one.

**1 John 3:19** This is how we will know that we belong to the truth and how we will be able to keep ourselves strong in his presence.

# Training Session 4:  A Warrior Is Wise

## Ecclesiastes 7

[25]I committed myself to understand, to learn, to search for
wisdom and explanations, and to understand both the evil
that is foolishness and the stupidity that is delusion.

**Focus of Training:**

1. What is Wisdom?

2. How does a Warrior achieve Wisdom?

3. Why should a Warrior be Wise?

4. What happens when someone operates without Wisdom?

5. Who do you think is Wise?

# Weapons

**Genesis 41:33** Therefore let Pharaoh select a wise, discerning person to place in charge over the land of Egypt.

**Genesis 41:39** "Since God has revealed all of this to you," Pharaoh told Joseph, "there is no one so wise and discerning as you.

**Deuteronomy 1:13** Choose for yourselves wise and discerning Men, known to your tribes, and appoint them as your leaders.

**Deuteronomy 1:15** So I chose leaders from your tribes, wise and respected Men, and I appointed them over you—comManders of thousands, hundreds, fifties, and tens.

**Deuteronomy 4:6** Observe them carefully, for this will show your wisdom and discernment in the eyes of people who'll listen to all these decrees. Then they'll say: 'Surely this great nation is a wise and discerning people.'

**Deuteronomy 16:19** You must not twist justice, show favoritism, or take bribes, because a bribe blinds the eyes of the wise and subverts the speech of the righteous.

**Deuteronomy 29:9** Therefore, keep the terms of this covenant, carrying them out so that you'll be wise in everything you do."

**Deuteronomy 32:29** O, that they were wise to understand this and consider their future!

**1 Samuel 12:15** But if you don't obey the LORD and rebel against the commandment of the LORD, then the LORD will turn against you as he did against your ancestors.

**2 Samuel 14:20** intending to change the outcome of this matter. Nevertheless, your majesty is wise, like the wisdom of the angel of God, to be aware of everything that's going on throughout the earth."

**1 Kings 2:9** But don't let him off unpunished, since you're a wise Man and you'll know what you need to do to him. Find a way that he dies in his old age by shedding his blood."

**1 Kings 3:12** look how I'm going to do precisely what you asked. I'm giving you a wise and discerning mind, so that there will have been no one like you before you and no one will arise after you like you.

**1 Kings 5:7** As soon as Hiram received the message from Solomon, he became so ecstatic that he exclaimed, "Blessed be the LORD today, who has given David a wise son to rule this great people!" Then he sent this message to Solomon:

**1 Kings 7:14** the son of a widow from the tribe of Naphtali, whose father was from Tyre. A bronze worker, he was wise, knowledgeable, and was skilled in all sorts of bronze working. He went to King Solomon and did all of his work.

**1 Kings 10:24** All the earth continued to seek audiences with Solomon so they could hear the wise things that God had put in his heart.

**2 Chronicles 9:23** All the kings of the earth continued to seek audiences with Solomon so they could hear the wise things that God had put in his heart.

**2 Chronicles 11:23** Rehoboam was wise to distribute some his children throughout all of the territories of Judah and Benjamin, placing them in all of the fortified cities. He allotted them abundant supplies of food and sought many wives for them.

**Esther 1:13** The king spoke to the wise Men who understood the times, for it was the king's custom to consult all those who understood law and justice.

**Job 9:4** He is wise in heart and strong in will—who can be stubborn against him and succeed?

**Job 12:13** With God is wisdom and strength; counsel and understanding belongs to him.

**Job 13:5** I wish you'd all just shut up. Then at least you would appear to be wise.

**Job 22:2** "Can a human being be useful to God, since he, who is wise, is sufficient to himself?

**Job 32:9** "The aged aren't always wise, nor do the elderly always understand justice.

**Job 34:2** "Listen to what I have to say, you wise Men! Pay attention to me, you educated people!

**Job 34:34** "Men of understanding, speak to me! Are any of you Men wise? Then listen to me!

**Job 37:24** Therefore humanity fears him, which none of the wise can quite comprehend."

**Psalms 48:14** For this God is our God forever and ever; he will be our guide even to the end.

**Psalms 19:7** The Law of the LORD is perfect, restoring life. The testimony of the LORD is steadfast, making foolish people wise.

**Psalms 73:24** You will guide me with your wise advice, and later you will receive me with honor.

**Psalms 94:8** Pay attention, you dull ones among the crowds! You fools! Will you ever become wise?

**Psalms 105:22** to discipline his rulers at will and make his elders wise.

**Psalms 107:43** Let whoever is wise observe these things, that they may comprehend the gracious love of the LORD.

**Proverbs 1:3** for acquiring the discipline that produces wise behavior, righteousness, justice, and upright living;

**Proverbs 1:5** Let the wise listen and increase their learning; let the person of understanding receive guidance

**Proverbs 3:7** Do not be wise in your own opinion. Fear the LORD and turn away from evil.

**Proverbs 3:35** The wise will inherit honor, but he holds fools up for ridicule.

**Proverbs 8:33** Listen to instruction and be wise. Don't ignore it.

**Proverbs 9:8** Don't rebuke a mocker or he will hate you. Rebuke a wise person, and he will love you.

**Proverbs 9:9** Counsel a wise Man, and he will be wiser still; teach a righteous Man, and he will add to his learning.

**Proverbs 9:12** If you are wise, your wisdom will assist you. If you mock, you alone will be held responsible.

**Proverbs 10:1** The proverbs of Solomon. A wise son brings joy to his father, but a foolish son grieves his mother.

**Proverbs 10:8** The wise person accepts commands, but the chattering fool will be brought down.

**Proverbs 10:14** Those who are wise store up knowledge, but when the fool speaks, destruction is near.

**Proverbs 11:29** Whoever troubles his household will inherit the wind, and the fool will be a servant to the wise.

**Proverbs 11:30** The fruit of the righteous is a tree of life, and the one who wins people is wise.

**Proverbs 12:8** A Man is praised because of his wise words, but the perverted mind will be despised.

**Proverbs 12:15** The lifestyle of the fool is right in his own opinion, but wise is the Man who listens to advice.

**Proverbs 12:18** Some speak rashly like the cutting of a sword, but what the wise say promotes healing.

**Proverbs 13:1** A wise son heeds a father's correction, but a mocker does not listen to rebuke.

**Proverbs 13:10** Arrogance only brings quarreling, but those receiving advice are wise.

**Proverbs 13:14** What the wise have to teach is a fountain of life and causes someone to avoid the snares of death.

**Proverbs 13:20** Whoever keeps company with the wise becomes wise, but the companion of fools suffers harm.

**Proverbs 14:3** What a fool says brings a rod to his back, but the words of the wise protect them.

**Proverbs 14:16** The wise person fears and turns away from evil, but a fool is reckless and overconfident.

**Proverbs 14:24** The crown of the wise is their wealth, but the stupidity of fools is just that—stupidity!

**Proverbs 14:35** The king approves the wise servant, but he is angry at anyone who acts shamefully.

**Proverbs 15:2** The wise speak, presenting knowledge appropriately, but fools spout foolishness.

**Proverbs 15:7** What the wise have to say disseminates knowledge, but it's not in the heart of fools to do so.

**Proverbs 15:12** The arrogant mocker never loves the one who corrects him; he will not inquire of the wise.

**Proverbs 15:24** The way of life leads upward for the wise so he may avoid Sheol below.

**Proverbs 15:31** Whoever listens to a life-giving rebuke will be at home among the wise.

**Proverbs 16:14** The king's wrath results in a death sentence, but whoever is wise will appease him.

**Proverbs 16:21** The wise-hearted person is told to be discerning, and pleasant speech promotes instruction.

**Proverbs 16:23** A wise person's thoughts control his words, and his speech promotes instruction.

**Proverbs 17:28** Even a fool is thought to be wise when he remains silent; he is thought to be prudent when he keeps his mouth shut.

**Proverbs 18:15** The mind of a discerning person gains knowledge, while the ears of wise people seek out knowledge.

**Proverbs 19:20** Listen to advice and accept discipline, and you'll be wise for the rest of your life.

**Proverbs 20:26** A wise king sifts the wicked, crushing them with the threshing wheel.

**Proverbs 21:11** When a mocker is punished, the fool gains wisdom; but when the wise is instructed, he receives knowledge.

**Proverbs 21:20** Precious treasures and oil are found where the wise live, but a foolish Man devours them.

**Proverbs 21:22** A wise Man attacks the city of the mighty, bringing down the fortress in which they trust.

**Proverbs 22:17** Pay attention and listen to the words of the wise, and apply your heart to my teaching,

**Proverbs 23:9** Don't speak when a fool is listening, because he'll despise your wise words.

**Proverbs 23:15** My son, if your heart is wise, my own heart will greatly rejoice.

**Proverbs 23:19** Listen, my son, and be wise, commit yourself to live God's way.

**Proverbs 23:24** The father of a righteous person will greatly rejoice; whoever fathers a wise son will be glad because of him.

**Proverbs 24:5** A wise Man is strong, and a knowledgeable Man grows in strength.

**Proverbs 24:6** For through wise counsel you will wage your war, and victory lies in an abundance of advisors.

**Proverbs 25:12** Like a gold earring and a necklace of pure gold is a wise reprover to a listening ear.

**Proverbs 26:5** Answer a fool according to his foolishness, or he will think himself to be wise.

**Proverbs 26:12** Do you see a Man who is wise in his own opinion? There's more hope for a fool than for him.

**Proverbs 27:11** Be wise, my son, and make me happy, so I can reply to anyone who insults me.

**Proverbs 28:11** The rich Man may be wise in his own opinion; but a discerning, poor Man sees through him.

**Proverbs 29:8** Scornful Men enflame a city, but the wise defuse anger.

**Proverbs 29:9** When a wise Man has a dispute with a fool, the fool either rages or laughs without relief.

**Proverbs 29:11** The fool vents all his feelings, but the wise person keeps them to himself.

**Proverbs 2:9** So I became great, greater than anyone who had lived before me in Jerusalem. Throughout all of this, I remained wise.

**Ecclesiastes 2:14** The wise use their eyes, but the fool walks in darkness. I also perceived that the same outcome affects them all.

**Ecclesiastes 4:13** A poor but wise youth is better than an old but foolish king who will no longer accept correction.

**Ecclesiastes 7:4** For the wise person thinks carefully when in mourning, but fools focus their thoughts on pleasure.

**Ecclesiastes 7:5** It is better to listen to a wise person's rebuke than to listen to the praise of fools.

**Ecclesiastes 7:11** Wise use of possessions is good; it brings benefit to the living.

**Ecclesiastes 7:19** Wisdom given as strength to a wise person is better than having ten powerful Men in the city.

**Ecclesiastes 7:28** Among the things I seek but have not found: one Man among a thousand I did find, but I have not found one Woman to be wise among all these.

**Ecclesiastes 8:1** Who is really wise? Who knows how to interpret this saying: "A person's wisdom improves his appearance, softening a harsh countenance."

**Ecclesiastes 8:5** Whoever obeys his commands will not experience harm, and the wise in heart will discern both the appropriate time and response.

**Ecclesiastes 9:17** The softly spoken words of the wise are to be heard rather than the shouts of a ruler of fools.

**Ecclesiastes 10:12** The words spoken by the wise are gracious, but the lips of a fool will devour him.

**Ecclesiastes 12:9** Moreover, besides being wise himself, the Teacher taught people what he had learned by listening, making inquiries, and composing many proverbs.

**Ecclesiastes 12:11** Sayings from the wise are like cattle prods and well fastened nails; this masterful collection was given by one shepherd.

**Isaiah 19:12** Where are your wise Men now? Let them tell you, let them make known what the LORD has planned against Egypt.

**Jeremiah 51:57** I'll make their leaders, their wise Men, their governors, their deputies, and their warriors drunk so that they sleep forever and don't wake up," declares the King whose name is the LORD of the Heavenly Armies.

**Daniel 2:21** It is God who alters the times and seasons, and he removes kings and promotes kings. He gives wisdom to the wise and knowledge to the discerning.

**Hosea 14:9** Whoever is wise, let him understand these things. Whoever is discerning, let him know them. For the ways of the LORD are right: the righteous follow his example, but the rebellious stumble in them.

**Matthew 23:34** "That is why I am sending you prophets, wise Men, and scribes. Some of them you will kill and crucify, and some of them you will whip in your synagogues and persecute from town to town.

**Matthew 24:45** "Who, then, is the faithful and wise servant whom his master has put in charge of his household to give the others their food at the right time?

**Matthew 25:2** Now five of them were foolish, and five were wise,

**Matthew 25:4** But the wise ones took flasks of oil with their lamps.

**Matthew 25:8** But the foolish ones told the wise, 'Give us some of your oil, because our lamps are going out!'

**Matthew 25:9** But the wise ones replied, 'No! There will never be enough for us and for you. You'd better go to the dealers and buy some for yourselves.'

**Romans 16:19** For your obedience has become known to everyone, and I am full of joy for you. But I want you to be wise about what is good, and innocent about what is evil.

**1 Corinthians 1:20** Where is the wise person? Where is the scholar? Where is the philosopher of this age? God has turned the wisdom of the world into nonsense, hasn't he?

**1 Corinthians 6:5** I say this to make you feel ashamed. Has it come to this, that there is not one person among you who is wise enough to settle disagreements between brothers?

**2 Corinthians 11:19** You are wise, so you will gladly be tolerant of fools.

**Ephesians 1:17** I pray that the God of our Lord Jesus, the Messiah, the most glorious Father, would give you a wise spirit, along with revelation that comes through knowing the Messiah fully.

**Ephesians 5:15** So, then, be careful how you live. Do not be unwise but wise.

**James 1:19** You must understand this, my dear brothers. Everyone should be quick to listen, slow to speak, and slow to get angry.

**James 3:13** Who among you is wise and understanding? Let him show by his noble conduct that his actions are done humbly and wisely.

# Training Session 5:  A Warrior Serves God Above All Else

## Matthew 22

[36]Teacher, which is the greatest commandment in the Law?
[37]Jesus told him, "You must love the Lord your God with all
your heart, with all your soul, and with all you mind.
[38]This is the greatest and most important commandant"
beside me like a great warrior.

**Focus of Training:**

1.  What does it mean to serve God above all else?

2.  Why should we serve God above all else?

3.  How does serving God above all else help fight the Spiritual Battle between Good and Evil?

4.  How does serving God above all else defend our family and community and attacks Evil?

5.  How do you ensure you're serving God above all else?

# Weapons

**Exodus 10:8** Moses and Aaron were brought back to Pharaoh and he told them, "Go, serve the LORD your God. But exactly who will go?"

**Exodus 10:26** And even our livestock must go with us. Not a hoof will be left behind because we will use some of them to serve the LORD our God, and until we get there we won't know what we need to serve the LORD."

**Exodus 20:5** You are not to bow down to them in worship or serve them; because I, the LORD your God, am a jealous God, punishing the children for the iniquity of the parents, to the third and fourth generations of those who hate me,

**Exodus 23:25** You are to serve the LORD your God, and he will bless your food and water, and I'll remove sickness from you.

**Deuteronomy 6:13** Fear the LORD your God, serve him, and make your oaths in his name.

**Deuteronomy 7:16** You are to utterly destroy everyone whom the LORD your God will deliver to you. Do not have pity on them nor serve their gods. Otherwise, they will become a snare for you."

**Deuteronomy 8:19** If you neglect the LORD your God, follow other gods, and serve and worship them, I testify to you today that you will certainly be destroyed.

**Deuteronomy 10:12** "Now Israel, what does the LORD your God desire from you? Only this: fear him, walk in all his ways, love him, serve him with all your heart and in all your life,

**Deuteronomy 10:20** You are to fear the LORD your God and serve him. Cling to him and swear by his name.

**Deuteronomy 11:13** "If you carefully observe the commands that I'm giving you today, to love the LORD your God and serve him with all your heart and soul,

**Deuteronomy 13:4** You must follow the LORD your God, fear him, observe his commandments, listen to his voice, serve him, and cling to him.

**Deuteronomy 18:5** For the LORD your God has chosen them and their descendants from among your tribes to stand and serve in the name of the LORD all their lives."

**Deuteronomy 28:47** "Because you didn't serve the LORD your God joyfully and wholeheartedly, despite the abundance of everything you have,

**Deuteronomy 28:48** you'll serve your enemies whom the LORD your God will send against you. You will serve in famine and in drought, in nakedness, and in lack of everything. They'll set a yoke of iron upon your neck until they have exterminated you.

**Deuteronomy 29:18** Be alert so there is no Man, Woman, family, or a tribe whose heart is turning

away from the LORD your God to go and serve the gods of those nations. "Be alert so there will be no root among you that produces poisonous and bitter fruit,

**Joshua 22:5** Only be very careful to keep the commands and the Law that Moses the servant of the LORD commanded you—that is, to love the LORD your God, to follow in all of his ways, to keep his commands, to stay close to him, and to serve him with all your heart and soul."

**Joshua 23:16** When you break the covenant of the LORD your God that he commanded you to obey by going to serve other gods and worship them, then the anger of the LORD will blaze against you, and you will perish quickly from this good land that he gave you."

**Joshua 24:18** The LORD expelled all the people before us, including the Amorites who lived in the land. Therefore, we also will serve the LORD, for he is our God."

**Joshua 24:24** The people replied, "We will serve the LORD our God and obey his voice."

**Judges 10:10** Then the Israelis cried out to the LORD and told him, "We have sinned against you because we have abandoned our God to serve the Baals."

**1 Samuel 12:14** If you fear the LORD, serve him, obey him, and don't rebel against the commandment of the LORD, then both you and the king who rules over you will truly follow the LORD your God.

**1 Chronicles 28:9** "Now as for you, my son Solomon, get to know the God of your father. Serve him with a sound heart and a devoted soul, because the LORD is searching every heart, every plan and thought. He will be found by you, assuming you are seeking him, but if you abandon him, he will abandon you forever.

**2 Chronicles 30:8** So don't be stiff-necked like your ancestors were. Instead, submit to the LORD, enter his sanctuary that he has sanctified forever, and serve the LORD your God so that he'll stop being angry with you.

**2 Chronicles 34:33** Josiah also removed all the detestable things from the territories that belonged to the people of Israel, and made everyone who lived in Israel to serve the LORD their God. For the rest of his life, they didn't abandon their quest to follow the LORD God of their ancestors.

**Jeremiah 5:19** When the people ask, 'Why has the LORD our God done all this to us?' you are to say to them, 'Just as you have forsaken me and served foreign gods in your land, so you will serve strangers in a land that is not yours.'"

**Ezekiel 20:20** You are to make my Sabbaths holy, and you are to let them serve as a sign between you and me, so that you may know that I am the LORD your God."

**Ezekiel 20:39** "And now, you house of Israel, this is what the Lord GOD says, 'Go ahead and serve your idols, both now and later, but later you'll listen to me, and you won't profane my sacred name again by your offerings and idols.

**Daniel 6:16** At this point, the king ordered Daniel brought in and thrown into the lions' pit. The king spoke to Daniel, "Your God, whom you serve constantly, will deliver you himself."

**Daniel 6:20** As he approached where Daniel was in the pit, he cried out to him in a voice filled with anguish, "Daniel, servant of the living God, has your God, whom you serve constantly, been able to deliver you from the lions?"

**Matthew 4:10** Then Jesus told him, "Go away, Satan! Because it is written, 'You must worship the Lord your God and serve only him.'"

**Matthew 6:24** "No one can serve two masters, because either he will hate one and love the other, or be loyal to one and despise the other. You cannot serve God and riches!"

**Matthew 6:33** But first be concerned about God's kingdom and his righteousness, and all of these things will be provided for you as well.

**Luke 4:8** But Jesus answered him, "It is written, 'You must worship the Lord your God and serve only him.'"

**Acts 7:7** 'But I will punish the nation they serve,' said God, 'and afterwards they will leave and worship me in this place.'

**2 Timothy 1:3** I constantly thank my God—whom I serve with a clear conscience, as my ancestors did—when I remember you in my prayers night and day,

**Revelation 19:5** A voice came from the throne, saying, "Praise our God, all who serve and fear him, from the least important to the most important."

# Training Session 6:  A Call to Action

## Revelation 6:2

And I saw, and behold a white horse: and he that sat on him had a bow; and a crown was given unto him:  and he went forth conquering, and to conquer.

**Focus of Training:**

1.  What are the characteristics of a Man who has chosen not to fight in the Spiritual Battle between Good and Evil?

2.  Why have some Men chosen not to fight in the Spiritual Battle between Good and Evil?

3.  How has refusing to fight empowered Evil?

4.  How has refusing to fight affected our families and communities?

5.  How does Warriors refusing to fight effect the future?

# Weapons

**Daniel 10:13** However, the prince of the kingdom of Persia opposed me for 21 days. Then—look! —Michael, one of the chief angels, came to assist me. I had been detained there near the kings of Persia.

**Daniel 12:1** "'At that time Michael will arise, the great prince who will stand up on behalf of your people, and a time of trouble will come like there has never been since nations began until that time. Also at that time, your people will be delivered—everyone who will have been written in the book.

**1 Corinthians 3: 13** the workmanship of each person will become evident, for the day of judgment will show what it is, because it will be revealed with fire, and the fire will test the quality of each person's action.

**Matthew 8:10** When Jesus heard this, he was amazed and told those who were following him, "I tell you with certainty, not even in Israel have I found this kind of faith!

**Matthew 8:26** He asked them, "Why are you afraid, you who have little faith?" Then he got up and rebuked the winds and the sea, and there was a great calm.

**Matthew 17:20** He told them, "Because of your lack of faith. I tell you with certainty, if you have faith like a grain of mustard seed, you can say to this mountain, 'Move from here to there,' and it will move, and nothing will be impossible for you.

**Matthew 21:12** Then Jesus went into the Temple, threw out everyone who was selling and buying in the Temple, and overturned the moneychangers' tables and the chairs of those who sold doves.

**Matthew 21:13** He told them, "It is written, 'My house is to be called a house of prayer,' but you are turning it into a hideout for bandits!"

**Matthew 21:15** But when the high priests and the scribes saw the amazing things that he had done and the children shouting in the Temple, "Hosanna to the Son of David," they became furious

**Matthew 21:21** Jesus answered them, "I tell you with certainty, if you have faith and do not doubt, not only will you be able to do what has been done to the fig tree, but you will also say to this mountain, 'Be removed and thrown into the sea,' and it will happen.

**Mark 4:40** He asked them, "Why are you such cowards? Don't you have any faith yet?"

**Mark 10:52** Jesus told him, "Go. Your faith has made you well." At once the Man could see again, and he began to follow Jesus down the road.

**Mark 11:15** When they came to Jerusalem, he went into the Temple and began to throw out those who were selling and those who were buying in the Temple. He overturned the moneychangers' tables and the chairs of those who sold doves.

**Mark 11:16** He wouldn't even let anyone carry a vessel through the Temple.

**Mark 11:17** Then he began to teach them: "It is written, is it not, 'My house is to be called a house of prayer for all nations'? But you have turned it into a hideout for bandits!"

**Mark 11:18** When the high priests and elders heard this, they began to look for a way to kill him, because they were afraid of him, since the whole crowd was amazed at his teaching.

**Mark 11:22** Jesus told his disciples, "Have faith in God!

**Luke 5:20** When Jesus saw their faith, he said, "Mister, your sins are forgiven."

**Luke 17:19** Then he told the Man, "Get up, and go home! Your faith has made you well."

**Luke 18:42** So Jesus told him, "See again! Your faith has made you well."

**Luke 19:45** Then Jesus went into the Temple and began to throw out those who were selling things.

**Luke 19:46** He told them, "It is written, 'My house is to be called a house of prayer,' but you have turned it into a hideout for bandits!"

**Luke 19:47** Then he began teaching in the Temple every day. The high priests, the scribes, and the leaders of the people kept looking for a way to kill him,

**John 2:15** After making a whip out of cords, he drove all of them out of the Temple, including the sheep and the cattle. He scattered the coins of the moneychangers and knocked over their tables.

**John 2:16** Then he told those who were selling the doves, "Take these things out of here! Stop making my Father's house a marketplace!"

**Acts 11:24** For he was a good Man, full of the Holy Spirit and faith. And so a large number of people was brought to the Lord.

**Acts 16:5** So the churches continued to be strengthened in the faith and to increase in numbers every day.

**Acts 26:18** You will help them understand and turn them from darkness to light and from Satan's control to God, so that their sins will be forgiven and they will receive a share among those who are sanctified by faith in me.'

**Romans 1:12** that is, that we may be mutually encouraged by each other's faith, both yours and mine.

**2 Corinthians 10:15** We are not boasting about work done by others that cannot be evaluated. On the contrary, we cherish the hope that your faith may continue to grow and enlarge our sphere of action among you until it overflows.

**2 Corinthians 13:5** Keep examining yourselves to see whether you are continuing in the faith. Test yourselves! You know, don't you, that Jesus the Messiah lives in you? Could it be that you are failing the test?

**Galatians 1:23** The only thing they kept hearing was this: "The Man who used to persecute us is now proclaiming the faith he once tried to destroy!"

**Galatians 6:1** Brothers, if a person is caught doing something wrong, those of you who are spiritual should restore that person gently. Watch out for yourself so that you are not tempted as well.

**Galatians 6:10** So then, whenever we have the opportunity, let's practice doing good to everyone, especially to the family of faith.

**Colossians 2:5** For although I am physically absent, I am with you in spirit, rejoicing to see how stable you are and how firm your faith in the Messiah is.

**1 Thessalonians 1:3** In the presence of our God and Father, we constantly remember how your faith is active, your love is hard at work, and your hope in our Lord Jesus the Messiah is enduring.

**1 Thessalonians 1:8** From you the word of the Lord has spread out not only in Macedonia and Achaia, but also in every place where your faith in God has become known. As a result, we do not need to say anything about it.

**1 Thessalonians 3:2** and send Timothy, our brother who works with us for God in the gospel of the Messiah, to strengthen and encourage you in your faith,

**1 Thessalonians 5: 14** We urge you, brothers, to admonish those who are idle, cheer up those who are discouraged, and help those who are weak. Be patient with everyone

**1 Timothy 4:6** If you continue to point these things out to the brothers, you will be a good servant of the Messiah Jesus, nourished by the words of the faith and the healthy teaching that you have followed closely.

**1 Timothy 6:12** Fight the good fight for the faith. Keep holding on to eternal life, to which you were called and about which you gave a good testimony in front of many witnesses.

**2 Timothy 4:7** I have fought the good fight. I have completed the race. I have kept the faith.

**Titus 1:1** From: Paul, a servant of God, and also an apostle of Jesus the Messiah, to bring the faith to those chosen by God, along with full knowledge of the truth that leads to godliness,

**Hebrews 13:7** Remember your leaders, those who have spoken God's word to you. Think about the impact of their lives, and imitate their faith.

**James 1:6** But he must ask in faith, without any doubts, for the one who has doubts is like a wave of the sea that is driven and tossed by the wind.

**James 2:26** For just as the body without the spirit is dead, so faith without actions is also dead.

**James 5:19** My brothers, if one of you wanders away from the truth and somebody brings him back, 20you may be sure that whoever brings a sinner back from his wrong path will save his soul from death and cover a multitude of sins.

# The Warrior Life Call to Action Plan

**Isaiah 6:8**

And I heard the voice of the Lord, saying, Whom shall I send, and who will go for us?
Then I said, Here am I; send me.

| Surrounds himself with Warriors. | Masters personal protection, weapons, and is physically fit. | Is mentally tough and perseveres. | Is wise. | Serves God above all else. |
| --- | --- | --- | --- | --- |
| Men's Bible study. | Join a gun range. | Quarterly "Stretch" events. | Study the Bible. | Set priorities. |
|  |  |  |  |  |
|  |  |  |  |  |
|  |  |  |  |  |
|  |  |  |  |  |

# Selected Warrior Resources

Warrior information https://thewarriorlife.wordpress.com
Ballistics http://en.wikipedia.org/wiki/Ballistics
BBQ http://en.wikipedia.org/wiki/Bbq
Beef Jerky http://en.wikipedia.org/wiki/Beef_jerky
Beer http://en.wikipedia.org/wiki/Beer
Browning http://www.browning.com
Children http://en.wikipedia.org/wiki/Children
Cigars http://en.wikipedia.org/wiki/Cigar
Combat Use of the Double-Edged Knife, Rex Applegate
http://www.aryanalibris.com/index.php?post/Applegate-Rex-Combat-use-of-the-double-edged-fighting-knife
Compasses http://en.wikipedia.org/wiki/Compass
Ferrari http://www.ferrari.com/Pages/Gateway.aspx?CountryId=88&CountryTitle=United+States
Fishing http://en.wikipedia.org/wiki/Fishing
Gold Bond http://www.goldbond.com
Handloading  http://en.wikipedia.org/wiki/Handloading
Holsters http://en.wikipedia.org/wiki/Holsters
Home Town Hotties http://www.maxim.com/girls/hometown-hotties
Hoppe's http://www.hoppes.com
Hot Sauce http://en.wikipedia.org/wiki/Hot_sauce
Hunting http://en.wikipedia.org/wiki/Hunting
Krav Maga http://www.kravmaga.com
Meat http://en.wikipedia.org/wiki/Meat
Mixed Martial Arts (MMA) http://en.wikipedia.org/wiki/Mixed_martial_arts
National Rifle Association www.nra.org
Nosler http://www.nosler.com
Old Spice http://www.oldspice.com/en-US/home-page.aspx
Relatives http://en.wikipedia.org/wiki/Relative
Remington http://www.remington.com
Sandwiches http://en.wikipedia.org/wiki/Sandwich
Smoked Oysters http://en.wikipedia.org/wiki/Smoked_oyster
Spam http://www.spam.com/#landing
Spartan™ Races http://www.spartan.com
Sports http://en.wikipedia.org/wiki/Sport
Springfield Armory http://www.springfield-armory.com
The Three Stooges http://en.wikipedia.org/wiki/The_three_stooges
Time http://en.wikipedia.org/wiki/Time
Top RaMen https://www.nissinfoods.com/products/TopRaMen
Trucks http://en.wikipedia.org/wiki/Truck
U. S. Army Civil Disturbances http://armypubs.army.mil/doctrine/DR_pubs/dr_a/pdf/atp3_39x33.pdf
U. S. Army Combat Training with Pistols, M9 and M11
http://armypubs.army.mil/doctrine/DR_pubs/dr_a/pdf/fm3_23x35.pdf
U. S. Army Combatives http://www.usarmycombatives.com
U. S. Army Counterinsurgency Operations http://fas.org/irp/doddir/army/fmi3-07-22.pdf
U. S. Army MarksManship Guide M16-/M4 Series Weapons
http://armypubs.army.mil/doctrine/DR_pubs/dr_a/pdf/fm3_22x9c1.pdf
U. S. Army Pocket Physical Fitness Guide
https://www.goarmy.com/content/dam/goarmy/downloaded_assets/pt_guide/pocket-pt-guide.pdf
U. S. Army Tactics in Counterinsurgency
http://armypubs.army.mil/doctrine/DR_pubs/dr_a/pdf/fm3_24x2.pdf
U. S. Marine Corps Martial Arts Program (MCMAP) file:///C:/aaaa/Offense/MCRP%203-02B%20PT%201.pdf
U. S. Marines Survival, Evasion, and Recovery
http://www.marines.mil/Portals/59/Publications/MCRP%203-02H%20Survival,%20Evasion%20and%20Recovery.pdf
United States Practical Shooters Association (USPSA) http://www.uspsa.org
Vienna Sausages http://www.armour-star.com/prod_vienna.asp

W.C. Fields http://en.wikipedia.org/wiki/W.C._Fields
Watches http://en.wikipedia.org/wiki/Watches
Weather http://en.wikipedia.org/wiki/Weather
Whiskey http://en.wikipedia.org/wiki/Whisky
Winchester http://www.winchesterguns.com
Wine http://en.wikipedia.org/wiki/Wine
Woman http://en.wikipedia.org/wiki/Woman

# Index